Max the
Sheepdog

'Max the Sheepdog'
An original concept by Cath Jones
© Cath Jones

Illustrated by Valeria Issa

Published by MAVERICK ARTS PUBLISHING LTD

Studio 3A, City Business Centre, 6 Brighton Road,

Horsham, West Sussex, RH13 5BB

© Maverick Arts Publishing Limited March 2019

+44 (0)1403 256941

A CIP catalogue record for this book is available at the British Library.

ISBN 978-1-84886-432-0

www.maverickbooks.co.uk

This book is rated as: Purple Band (Guided Reading)

Max the Sheepdog

By **Cath Jones**

Illustrated by **Valeria Issa**

Max thought Mum was the best sheepdog in the whole world. He loved to watch her rounding up the sheep, bringing them safely back to the farm.

Every day, Max asked, "Mum, can

I help round up the sheep?"

But the answer was always the same:

"Not today, Max. You dash around too much

to be a sheepdog. You'll only scare the sheep!"

5

Max felt sad. He was sure he could be a brilliant sheepdog. If only Mum would give him a chance! 'I know,' thought Max. 'I'll practice my rounding up skills while Mum is at work.'

First he tried to round up his brothers

and sisters. It wasn't that easy!

'Perhaps spiders might be easier to round up,' thought Max. He set off for the barn to sort out all the spiders. DASH, JUMP, ZOOM!

He chased the spiders round and round the barn.

"SLOW DOWN!" yelled the spiders. Then they

rolled up and hid in high corners!

Max let out a long sigh. 'Being a sheepdog is

really quite tricky,' he thought.

But Max was not ready to give up. He raced round the farm looking for something else to round up.

Suddenly, he noticed that someone had left the farm gate wide open! This was his chance to show Mum what a fantastic sheepdog he could be...

Max ran out of the gate and up the track.

He raced into a field and stared at some sheep.

"Baaaah," cried the sheep.

"Woof!" barked Max.

Then he dashed towards them.

The sheep fled!

"Come back!" barked Max. His barking echoed up the valley, all the way to where Mum was working. Mum came running!

"Max!" said Mum. "A sheepdog must watch and wait and creep. You're in too much of a hurry to round up the sheep. Go back to the farm, son, and leave the sheep in peace."

Max tried not to cry as he made his way

back down the track.

He was almost back at the farm when

he spotted a sheep all alone.

'That sheep must be lost,' thought Max.

I must help it get back to its family!

DASH, JUMP, ZOOM!

The sheep took one look at Max and fled!

"Wait! Come back," barked Max.

But the sheep ran across the field, down

the hill, all the way to the jetty.

Max ran as fast as he could to catch up

with the sheep. He sped down the hill,

faster and faster and faster.

"Uh-oh!" Max yelped as he ran straight off

the edge into the sea! SPLASH!

Luckily Max was a good swimmer.

Lots of fish darted past. 'Maybe I can round up the fish,' thought Max. But they were even trickier than the sheep.

Above, seagulls began to shriek and squawk.
Max tried rounding up the seagulls too but
they were impossible, much too flappy and
far too high.

After all that dashing around, Max began to feel very tired. He climbed onto a large rock and lay down for a rest. Suddenly, a lifeboat came speeding across the top of the waves.

"Pick up that dog!" yelled a woman on board.

It was fantastic fun on the lifeboat!

The boat dashed through the water, crashing through the waves. The lifeboat was almost back in the harbour when...

...a blanket of white fog crept over the sea.

The boat slowed right down.

Max looked up at the cliffs but the fog

hid everything from view.

He dashed to the front of the boat to be a

lookout. He searched for rocks and boats

that were in danger because of the fog.

The lifeboat crept round and round. Together,

Max and the lifeboat rounded up all the boats.

They kept all the boats safe.

Finally, the fog cleared and they headed back to shore. Max spotted Mum waiting for him on the jetty. He waved.

"Mum! I've been helping the lifeboat round up all the boats," barked Max. "I'm not a sheepdog, I'm a SHIPDOG!"

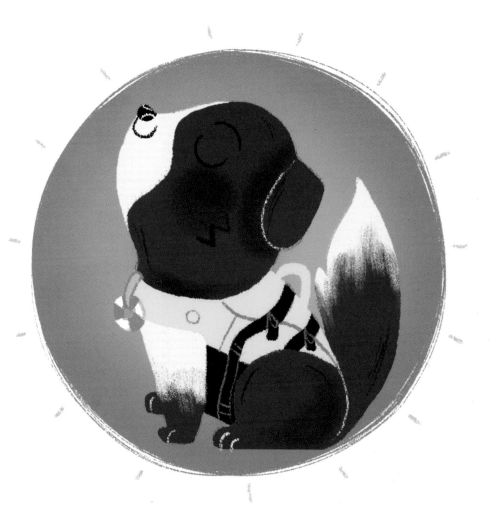

Mum barked happily. She was very proud of Max!

Quiz

1. Who does Max want to be like?

a) The sheep

b) A boat

c) His mum

2. Where does Max try to sort out the spiders?

a) In the barn

b) On the jetty

c) In the sea

3. Max's mum says, "A sheepdog must watch and wait and _____?"

a) Eat

b) Creep

c) Run

4. Why are the cliffs hidden from view?

a) Because there is fog

b) Because the waves are too high

c) Because there are rocks in the way

5. What does Max round up in the end?

a) The fish

b) The boats

c) The sheep

Turn over for answers

Book Bands for Guided Reading

The Institute of Education book banding system is a scale of colours that reflects the various levels of reading difficulty. The bands are assigned by taking into account the content, the language style, the layout and phonics. Word, phrase and sentence level work is also taken into consideration.

Maverick Early Readers are a bright, attractive range of books covering the pink to white bands. All of these books have been book banded for guided reading to the industry standard and edited by a leading educational consultant.

To view the whole Maverick Readers scheme, visit our website at
www.maverickearlyreaders.com

Or scan the QR code above to view our scheme instantly!

Quiz Answers: 1c, 2a, 3b, 4a, 5b